OVERCOMER
*Mastering Defining Moments Through
Prayer and Fasting*

OVERCOMER
Mastering Defining Moments Through Prayer and Fasting

C. Jai Graham

The Author's Pen

USA

The Author's Pen, LLC
PO Box 720798
Houston, TX 77272
www.tapwriting.com

Scriptures marked NIV are taken from the NEW INTERNATIONAL VERSION (NIV): Scripture taken from THE HOLY BIBLE, NEW INTERNATIONAL VERSION ®. Copyright© 1973, 1978, 1984, 2011 by Biblica, Inc.™. Used by permission of Zondervan.

Scripture marked NLT are taken from the Holy Bible, New Living Translation, copyright ©1996, 2004, 2015 by Tyndale House Foundation. Used by permission of Tyndale House Publishers, Inc., Carol Stream, Illinois 60188. All rights reserved.

Scriptures marked AMP are taken from the Amplified® Bible (AMP), Copyright © 2015 by The Lockman Foundation Used by permission. www.Lockman.org

Scripture marked NKJV are taken from the New King James Version®. Copyright © 1982 by Thomas Nelson. Used by permission. All rights reserved.

Scriptures marked as ESV are taken from The ESV Global Study Bible®, ESV® Bible Copyright © 2012 by Crossway. All rights reserved.

Overcomer: Mastering Defining Moments Through Prayer and Fasting. -- 1st Print ed.
ISBN 978-1-948248-08-2

This book is dedicated first and foremost to
My Lord and Savior, Jesus Christ.
Without You, there is no me!

To my husband and children, I want you to know with all that is in you, NOTHING is impossible with Jesus, no matter your age, your background, or how many times you had to fall and get back up and keep it moving!

God doesn't give up on you, so don't give up on Him or yourself.

CONTENTS

Have you ever been in a season of life where it seemed as if it was one thing after another? You think you may have a handle on *this* and then *that* sprung up catching you by surprise and you're screaming "I haven't even handled this issue yet?"

Many times, we cannot see it while we're in it, but when I proclaim that God is good, I mean it. I am a living testimony that what he leads you to and through, he will bring you out of. And it's for His glory!

I am from Florida, but because I joined the military right after high school, I was away for a number of years. Upon my return to Florida, I was looking for a place of employment and applied everywhere my qualifications (certified medical assistant) afforded me. I was not having much movement.

I decided to just start applying anywhere, whether I qualified or not. One day, I applied for a position at a private college as a medical assistant instructor. The next day, they called me in for an interview. I was going bananas and not in a good way. I was shocked that they *actually* called me, and I was afraid because I had no teaching experience.

I went in for the interview and was offered the position. It was a part time position paying the same income I was making while working full time in Tennessee. It was perfect for me, as I was planning to go back to school the upcoming semester.

Due to other defining moments, I had to quit school to work fulltime. The opportunity opened right up when I needed it. God is good, isn't he? I was working as an instructor for a little over five years when I was called into the office and told I would be reduced to part time. This was not good. I had a house and a family. We managed, and I stayed on part time praying for an opportunity to go back fulltime.

News came that the college was going to be bought out by a nonprofit organization and I was hoping this would be my opportunity to get back to a fulltime position. I even said to myself and my husband that if they did not offer me fulltime, I was leaving.

I'm chuckling as I type this because I thought I was really serious and brave enough to do what I said I was going to do.

They came, they bought, and they moved on. I was still working for the new organization on a part time basis. I settled in that place and was still hoping and praying for a different outcome.

When that different outcome came, I was prepared for it, but I wasn't. Let me explain.

One Monday night, I was home, doing nothing out of the ordinary. All of a sudden, I started feeling as if I needed to stay home the next day and miss work. I started to reason with myself saying things like, *"I'm not sick. I don't need to play sick tomorrow. I don't have anything to do."* I didn't think much of it and went on about my night.

I woke up Tuesday morning, and was getting my day started as I did regularly. I started to have that feeling again concerning staying home and began reasoning with myself. I ended up just following the unction to stay home.

After everyone left the house, I went into my prayer time and it was different this time. I was being ministered to on a level I had not experienced, being encouraged, loved being poured into me, just a feeling of peace and the sense that God was in control.

Later that afternoon, a friend from work called and shared with me that a few of our coworkers had been laid off and escorted off campus earlier that day. As soon as I heard the news, I instantly knew that after almost seven years with this organization, I was one of the people who, had I been there that day was to receive the news. I would not have been prepared for it. Who knows how I would have reacted, who would have been adversely affected, and the impression I would have left.

One of the most important things I had to consider was that I was already going through some tough things, and who knows but God what that would have done to me being blindsided with yet another blow to my life.

I thank God for thinking enough of me to prepare me for this moment and for the plans he had, not only for me, but the people who were watching how I handled the news. By the time I arrived to work the next day, I was going through the day like it was a movie. I had seen it a thousand times and I could've recited the lines of the actors myself! I was flowing through each moment and I knew ahead of time what was happening and how to respond. I saw the goodness and the compassion of God every step of the way.

I was in awe. I saw how he removed my friend from the work environment early in the day, so she would not be there when they finally told me the news, because she would not have acted right! She needed to see me handle it with grace so that she could handle it with grace. She needed to hear and see me and my faith at work, so she wouldn't unknowingly create doubt and fear in me. She needed to see my strength so that she could support me in the way I needed to be supported as I transitioned from one place to another.

I was formally laid off that day, but I had to teach out the semester. For two weeks and a small severance, I was to be faith in action; not pretension, I said *action*.

People were both amazed and confused by my reaction in faith. They were reminding me that they understood my faith, but I still needed to pay the bills, or asking me what my next move was because the bills would be stacking up as I put my faith in God to provide for me. I was responding to them from a place of peace and assurance that God was indeed taking care of me. I could see my circumstance beyond the surface of needing the security of employment.

God needed me to trust him, to walk in faith, and to be obedient. Had I not listened and stayed home that day, the responses and reactions of others, and well-meaning attempts to comfort me would have potentially caused me to abort the upcoming process, get out of the will of God and delay my destiny.

Once I got through those two weeks and home to really allow this new defining moment to sink in, I was like, "Ok God, now what?" It hasn't been easy, I've done my own getting out of the will of God and delaying my destiny, but God has been there every step of the way, putting me back on course and keeping me when I didn't know what to do or how to respond.

This journal was birthed during this process by allowing God to continue to navigate my life's path through the work he continues to do in me, so he can do a work through me. I am grateful to be used and I am mastering the defining moments that contribute to me becoming all that God has created me to be.

My sincere prayer is that you will allow him to do the same for you and that this journal is a tremendous guide for you along the way.

This Book's Purpose

What I have discovered as a result of being a follower of Christ is that this status does not exempt me from experiencing trials and hardships (I like to call them defining moments) in life. As a matter of fact, as I committed to my walk with Christ and began to study the bible, I found a few scriptures in the Word of God corroborating this very discovery.

In St John 16:33, Jesus tells us that in this world, we will have trials, tribulation, distress and frustration, but be of good cheer, courageous, confident and certain. Why? Because He has overcome the world!

This means for me, that although I am going to experience many circumstances that may cause me hurt and pain (sometimes extreme), may cause me to lose some people or things, may cause me to change or alter the course or path that I set out for myself and maybe my loved ones, I can have faith, be joyful; I can have peace, and continue boldly and courageously on my walk with Christ because from the beginning victory is mine and in the end, I will triumph!

Jesus has already signed, sealed, and delivered my expected end (a victorious, abundant life and eternal salvation).

Upon this discovery fellow child of God, it was revealed to me that the difference between followers of Christ and the rest of the world is how we respond to the trials, the tribulation, the distress and the frustration. I hinted to this briefly just a moment ago. Let's look at St John 16:33 NIV which reads, "I have told you these things, so that in me you may have peace. In this world you will have trouble. But take heart! I have overcome the world."

What instructions did Jesus give to us?

Now, let us study another scripture. James, the half-brother of Jesus, instructs us in James 1:2-4 to count it all joy (be of good cheer, confident, be certain) when we fall into various trials, knowing that the testing of our faith produces patience. James goes on to say that we should let patience have its perfect work in our lives so that we may be perfect and complete, lacking nothing.

Trials and hardships in life build our faith, grow our dependence on God, mature us in the spirit, producing a lifestyle that we do not only wear on a t-shirt or profess with our mouth, but can be witnessed by others who wish to know and experience the presence of God and live a victorious lifestyle of their own. Our good works, not our good words, are to be a shining light for others that they may glorify the Father, who is in heaven (Matthew 5:16).

I know you have been waiting (patiently, right?) for me to reveal to you the reason this book exists. The birth of this book came from my own storms, hardships, frustration, and the need for God to show me how to obey His Word. I needed God to instruct me on how to be of good cheer, count it all joy, and grow my faith and dependence on Him.

My prayer is that this book helps you:

- To love God and others with all your heart (Matthew 22:37-39),

- To continually move forward (Philippians 3:12-14),

- To mature in the ways of Christ (Galatians 5:22-26),

- To guard your heart (Proverbs 4:23),

- To stay pure and clean before God that you may continue to be used for His glory (Romans 12:1),

- To overcome negative thoughts (Ephesians 4:26-27).

Allow the Spirit of God to tailor your experience and relationship with Him, that He may help you in ways that are unique to you and your trials, hardships, storms and frustrations (defining moments) in life.

This Book's Conception

Let me introduce and define the 4 P's and briefly explain how they came about.

Pray
To speak to God especially in order to give thanks or to seriously and in faith ask for something.

Purge
To rid of whatever is impure or undesirable; to clear out or wipe away legally by atonement or other suitable action.

Prepare
To put things or oneself in proper condition or readiness.

Position
The manner of being placed in a proper or appropriate place. A place or condition to be occupied as with bodily posture or attitude.

During the revelation and process of putting together this journal, I was dealing with some difficult times in my own life. For years I had been going through trial after trial after trial. They seemed to be coming out of nowhere. I am not talking about small stuff, I'm talking about life altering, and life shattering if you let it type stuff. Honestly, I felt at times like what I was going through was going to cause me to go under, never to return. I was broken, completely overwhelmed, emotionally unstable, undone, and I couldn't seem to regain my footing.

Every area, and I do mean every area of my life was under attack where I experienced loss, damage, lack, distrust, doubt, fear, you name it, it was there. I did not have a clue as to how to handle any of it, I was confused as to what was happening, and although I did my best to resolve issues and stay strong, I didn't have any answers.

My world was upside down! I do want to say that in the beginning, my relationship with God was not a consistent one. I did make a decision at some point to commit to living a God-first life. I had been praying, attending church regularly, tithing; the works and still saw no relief. I was going through every kind of emotion you can think of and I just was not able to find any peace or resolve within myself.

In December 2015, I decided that I was going to prepare myself for the upcoming New Year. I wanted a fresh start and I did not want 2016 to be like every year before. I decided that I would go on a fast to help me get that fresh start, even if it was only in my mind. I didn't know how I was going to change or how my circumstances were going to change, but I desperately needed life to be different.

I resolved that I could at least bring my mind (and my emotions) under control, focus on God a little more, and increase my expectation for the year ahead. God had much, much more up His sleeve and my goodness; I was not prepared for what was to come.

Immediately, on the first day, God showed up and began to deal with me about the trials I was going through and how I didn't handle them appropriately. He gave me the 4 P's and instructions to follow over the next 21 days concerning them and how to apply them. This process opened me up to receive much more than peace and the wherewithal to handle the storm that was not going to let up any time soon.

I mentioned previously the intention of trials and hardships in our lives and that they are inevitable. But, the real question is how do we handle them when they come? We put the 4 P's in motion is what we do!

Later, I will provide an example of what Pray, Purge, Prepare, and Position looks like in practical application.

For now, we will take a detailed look at each of the 4 Principles and related scriptural references to ensure understanding, which will prove to help you be successful in triumphing over defining moments of your life.

I'm excited to take the journey with you and I know our heavenly Father is smiling down as you take charge of your life through praying, purging, preparing, and positioning yourself.

My only other advice is:

- Be in expectation and believe what you pray when you pray.
- Be in obedience and do not delay.
- Be honest with yourself and God about everything.
- Ask for forgiveness where you have erred.
- Accept God's love and His correction.
- Forgive yourself for your contribution.
- Celebrate your successes along the way.
- Commit more time to the process as needed and as you feel led.
- Bring someone along with you who will not only encourage you, but can benefit by doing this with you.

CHAPTER ONE

PRAY

1 Thessalonians 5:16-18 Amplified Bible (AMP)

Rejoice always *and* delight in your faith; be unceasing *and* persistent in prayer; in every situation [no matter what the circumstances] be thankful *and* continually give thanks *to God*; for this is the will of God for you in Christ Jesus.

Pray

Prayer is essential to the Christian's life and apart from it, there is no possible way to have an intimate relationship with God. Prayer gives us the opportunity to thank God for the blessings we receive on a daily basis, to shower Him with praise for who He is in our lives and worship Him for His priceless gift of Jesus Christ to us who wiped away all of our sins and bestowed life through the gift of grace.

Prayer also affords us the privilege to speak with God; to talk with Him about what is going on in our lives (although he already knows), to share how we are feeling about ourselves and life (He wants us to talk with Him about those things, just as we would talk to a trusted friend), to make specific requests of Him for our needs and desires, and to invite Him in on the details of every part of our life to guide and direct us in His perfect plan for our life (Jeremiah 29:11).

Things to Consider Regarding Prayer:

The Call to Pray and Fast
Matthew 17:21 New King James Version (NKJV)

However, this kind does not go out except by prayer and fasting."

Important and Primary Part of Prayer
Psalm 100:4 New King James Version (NKJV)

Enter into His gates with thanksgiving, and into His courts with praise. Be thankful to Him, and bless His name.

Philippians 4:6-7 New Living Translation (NLT)

Don't worry about anything; instead, pray about everything. Tell God what you need, and thank him for all he has done. Then you will experience God's peace, which exceeds anything we can understand. His peace will guard your hearts and minds as you live in Christ Jesus.

Timothy 2:1-2 New Living Translation (NLT)

I urge you, first of all, to pray for all people. Ask God to help them; intercede on their behalf, and give thanks for them. Pray this way for kings and all who are in authority so that we can live peaceful and quiet lives marked by godliness and dignity.

Matthew 5:44 New King James Version (NKJV)

But I say to you, love your enemies, bless those who curse you, do good to those who hate you, and pray for those who spitefully use you and persecute you.

James 5:16 Amplified Bible (AMP)

Therefore, confess your sins to one another [your false steps, your offenses], and pray for one another, that you may be healed *and* restored. The heartfelt *and* persistent prayer of a righteous man (believer) can accomplish much [when put into action and made effective by God—it is dynamic and can have tremendous power].

It is a command and a vital tool for us to pray. We are to pray for ourselves, our loved ones, and even our enemies! We all are God's children and in need of prayer. Some circumstances we face in life, will require prayer and fasting.

The purpose of these thought questions is to give you a general idea of where you currently stand with your defining moments, what God is saying to you even before you begin the fast, and pray.

Pray

Do you pray often? If not, why?

After reading the section on prayer, what new information, knowledge, and understanding has God revealed to you regarding prayer?

What new instructions has God given you regarding your view of or approach to prayer?

Which scripture about prayer spoke to you the loudest?

Create a prayer outlining your favorite scripture to use during your fast.

CHAPTER TWO

PURGE

2 Timothy 2:21 Amplified Bible (AMP)

So whoever cleanses himself [from what is ignoble and unclean, who separates himself from contact with contaminating and corrupting influences] will [then himself] be a vessel set apart and useful for the honorable and noble purposes, consecrated and profitable to the master, fit and ready for any good work.

Purge

Why is purging important?

Whether good, bad, or indifferent, we can accumulate within us, feelings, thoughts, and actions that, over time, can dictate what we believe, how we show up in life and the path we ultimately take. These accumulations affect our relationships, jobs, sense of self and our attitudes in general. For example, if we are caught in the rain while driving, our vehicles get wet, right? Even after the rain stops, our vehicle dries, and time has elapsed, we can still see the residue of the rain.

Our experiences in life are much the same. Years after a relationship has ended, we can still carry residue of the hurt, distrust, disappointment, and anger accumulated while in the relationship. Jealousy, competition, strife, and division can create the same feelings we experienced on a job we had ten years ago when we were overlooked for that promotion or worked for a boss who abused their authority.

When you think to yourself, "Why can't I push back from the table or quit late night snacking when I know I shouldn't be doing it?" Some of you may have asked yourself. It may be an unconscious coping mechanism related to the residue the job or other situation left on you.

A major loss, trial, or defining moment in our lives can take root in our minds and hearts and over time if they're not dealt with properly, will take on a mind of their own. This can create a life that is unstable, not pleasing to God, and rob us of the quality of life we truly desire, and that God desires for us as well. These trials can also provide an opportunity for the enemy to have his way with us if we're unaware and not careful how we handle them. Not dealing with issues or not dealing with them properly, can affect us in many ways that we may not always be able to identify.

Purging allows God to search us and bring to the forefront things that we need to confront, be honest about, confess and repent for, and allows Him to commune with us as we truly are. Whether others hurt you, you hurt yourself, or the hardships of life seem to have gotten the best of you, God wants the real you.

Purging is also proactive. In God bringing to the forefront those things you have correctly identified and are to confront, following, are instructions to carry out, as you are an active participant in the process.

If there is a phone number to be deleted, pictures to throw away, memories to let go of, or counseling to seek out, then God expects us to follow through with what he instructs us to do to effectively purge and be ready for the next level of the process to healing and wholeness in our lives. His ultimate purpose, as I'm sure you know but may need to be reminded of, is to flow through you unhindered as he uses you to do for others what he is doing in you.

Psalm 51:6–7 English Standard Version (ESV)

"Behold, you delight in truth in the inward being, and you teach me wisdom in the secret heart. Purge me with hyssop, and I shall be clean; wash me, and I shall be whiter than snow."

Proverbs 4: 23 New International Version (NIV)

Above all else, guard your heart, for everything you do flows from it.

1 Peter 5:7-8 New Living Translation (NLT)

Give all your worries and cares to God, for he cares about you. Stay alert! Watch out for your great enemy, the devil. He prowls around like a roaring lion, looking for someone to devour.

Romans 12:2 New Living Translation (NLT)

Don't copy the behavior and customs of this world, but let God transform you into a new person by changing the way you think. Then you will learn to know God's will for you, which is good and pleasing and perfect.

John 4:24 New Living Translation (NLT)

For God is Spirit, so those who worship him must worship in spirit and in truth."

Purge

After reading the section on purge, what new information, knowledge, and understanding has God revealed to you regarding purge?

As you were learning more about purging, what emotion, feeling, behavior, person, or situation immediately came to your mind that you need to purge?

List two steps you can take immediately, to be proactive in purging the element you listed in the previous question.

Which scripture about purge spoke to you the loudest?

Create a prayer outlining your favorite scripture to use during your fast.

CHAPTER THREE

PREPARE

James 2:18 New Living Translation (NLT)

Now someone may argue, "Some people have faith; others have good deeds." But I say, "How can you show me your faith if you don't have good deeds? I will show you my faith by my good deeds."

Prepare

Preparation is critical to us moving beyond our current state, circumstances, and to the next level. After the purging process, we have to replace what was purged with something else. We are getting rid of what doesn't work and replacing it with what does work. Preparation is also a demonstration of our faith in God, that He hears us and that prayers will be answered. We are letting God know that we heard His *Yes and Amen*, and now we are going to do our part and be patient as our preparedness meets His timing.

Preparation may show up in various ways and depending on your circumstances and the unique way in which God wishes to have you prepare. It will look different from one situation to the next, as well from one person to another.

For these reasons, it is not always wise to seek opinions and counsel from people about how to best handle your defining moments. People may be well-meaning and want the best for you; however, unless they are assigned to your life and are journeying with you through the process, their advice will not align with God's path and plan for you. Their perspective will be limited, based upon their experiences, or what they know about your personality and how you have handled situations in the past.

Those who are assigned to you and will journey with you will hear from God concerning you as well. Their heart is pure toward you, they are sensitive to the Spirit on your behalf, and they pray with you and for you.

God's plan for you is to do life his way because his way is the best. He sees what we cannot see and knows what we do not know.

It's not wise to rely solely on previous situations and problem-solving skills used at that time, because as we seek God and His will in our life situations, He can very well tell us to do something different than what we may have or will come up with on our own. You may have had two people in your life that mistreated you in a similar way. One, you may have cut off whereas God may tell you to remain in relationship with the other person until He releases you or change the circumstances surrounding the relationship. Whatever the reason, there is something God is trying to accomplish when He asks us to do something, especially when it is contrary to what we would do on our own.

Often, we encounter some of our defining moments because we listened to someone else or had to have our own way in a situation. You can tell me the truth, I won't tell anyone! Thank God, for He can turn any situation around for our good and His glory.

Now don't misunderstand me, God can and will use people, however, it is at His direction and they must be mature in Christ and will always encourage you to seek God and His ways. Their counsel will be biblical, confirm or otherwise be in agreeance, letting you know that you are on the right track. Be in prayer and seek God for guidance in choosing someone to talk with and get advice about how to best handle your defining moment.

During your prayer and fasting, you will hear God talking with you if you're listening.

After all, that's the reason for the process, to hear what God has to say and gain revelation as to what He wants you to do, right? He gives us bits and pieces of information, not the whole roll out or blue print. When He does give us little tasks to complete and instructions to follow, He expects us to obey them. Completely obey them, whether we agree or not, feel like it, or even understand. It's not enough to have faith in God and His ability to help us in our time of need. Action is required on our end.

Matthew 12: 43-45 English Standard Version (ESV)

When the unclean spirit has gone out of a person, it passes through waterless places seeking rest, but finds none. Then it says, 'I will return to my house from which I came.' And when it comes, it finds the house empty, swept, and put in order. Then it goes and brings with it seven other spirits more evil than itself, and they enter and dwell there, and the last state of that person is worse than the first. So also will it be with this evil generation."

Isaiah 43:19 New Living Translation (NLT)

For I am about to do something new. See, I have already begun! Do you not see it? I will make a pathway through the wilderness. I will create rivers in the dry wasteland.

1 Corinthians 10:13 New Living Translation (NLT)

The temptations in your life are no different from what others experience. And God is faithful. He will not allow the temptation to be more than you can stand. When you are tempted, he will show you a way out so that you can endure.

James 2:17 New International Version (NIV)

In the same way, faith by itself, if it is not accompanied by action, is dead.

Proverbs 6:6-8 English Standard Version (ESV)

Go to the ant, O sluggard; consider her ways, and be wise. Without having any chief, officer, or ruler, she prepares her bread in summer and gathers her food in harvest.

Prepare

After reading the section on prepare, what new information, knowledge, and understanding has God revealed to you regarding prepare?

What instruction(s) has God already given you regarding preparing for the next level he's taking you?

Have you completed them? If not, why?

Which scripture about prepare spoke to you the loudest?

Create a prayer outlining your favorite scripture to use during your fast.

CHAPTER FOUR

POSITION

2 Peter 3:17 New International Version (NIV)

Therefore, dear friends, since you have been forewarned, be on your guard so that you may not be carried away by the error of the lawless and fall from your secure position.

Position

When talking about position, we are not looking only at physical position, but also a spiritual position. As with the other P's there are many scriptures in the bible that support the fact that positioning is important. Prayer and fasting, as it relates to positioning, puts us in a place to first and foremost, hear from God. We cannot and should not want to move forward in any situation without guidance from God.

Looking beyond physical things, positioning helps us regroup and set our eyes on what God reveals during the fast. Position, which can take place physically, in our mind, our actions, our faith, and more, opens way for a new standing as we complete our fast for God to do something new in our life.

Whether you are a new Christian or have been walking with God for years, there should be a constant renewing, positioning, as well as reminder of our place in Christ, in heavenly places, and in the various areas we occupy on earth. We can forget sometimes. We can get stuck sometimes. I find that when we find ourselves stuck at some point and we're trying to get out of circumstances and situations but can't seem to, it may be because God wants to do something new, but instead of seeking Him for guidance and His will for our life, we resort to our same tactics, solutions and strategies.

Positioning in any form as guided by God does not mean it will feel good, look good, or sound good. Do not rely on your physical senses to dictate whether you are in the right position, and more importantly, not abort a position because you don't think it is God who has you there. The truth of God's word, personal revelation and promises He's given are the foundation of your moving to and staying in position.

Look at Joseph. God revealed to him in a dream that he would be in a certain position that promised to be one of authority, status, and blessing. Along the way to that promise of position, Joseph found himself in a pit, sold into slavery, accused of adultery with another man's wife and thrown into prison. This may not have been the process Joseph had in mind, nor would have signed up for it if he was told of this process (Thank God he doesn't tell us everything!), but they were positions also, each one serving its own purpose. And note, all of these positions led him to the ultimate place God had for him as Egypt's second in command.

Colossian 3:1-3 New Living Translation (NLT)

Since you have been raised to new life with Christ, set your sights on the realities of heaven, where Christ sits in the place of honor at God's right hand. Think about the things of heaven, not the things of earth.

Romans 12:2 New Living translation (NLT)

Don't copy the behavior and customs of this world, but let God transform you into a new person by changing the way you think. Then you will learn to know God's will for you, which is good and pleasing and perfect.

Ephesians 6:13 New International Version (NIV)

Therefore, put on the full armor of God, so that when the day of evil comes, you may be able to stand your ground, and after you have done everything, to stand.

Hebrews 11:6 New International Version (NIV)

And without faith it is impossible to please God, because anyone who comes to him must believe that he exists and that he rewards those who earnestly seek him.

Genesis 12:1 New Living Translation (NIV)

The LORD had said to Abram, "Leave your native country, your relatives, and your father's family, and go to the land that I will show you.

Psalm 37:23 New Living Translation (NLT)

The LORD directs the steps of the godly. He delights in every detail of their lives.

Proverbs 3:5-6 New Living Translation (NLT)

Trust in the LORD with all your heart; do not depend on your own understanding. Seek his will in all you do, and he will show you which path to take.

Now that we've had an opportunity to explore the 4 P's in detail, allow me to share my thoughts concerning defining moments before we move on to a list of examples.

What I have learned over time is that when I find myself in the same situation over and over again, it's probably best that I quit looking at the situation itself or the person/people involved and turn to look at and examine myself.

Even though we try to learn from our mistakes in an effort to do it differently the next time, we may miss some critical points of change because we usually approach the situation from a topical or symptom-like vantage point. What I mean is that we will look at a behavior or habit and try to change it or break it, rather than deal with the root of the behavior or habit. We don't always ask ourselves, "what is causing me to indulge in this behavior or why have I developed this habit?" We focus on the behavior or habit and try to will ourselves not to do "that" again. We will keep facing the issue until we find out what needs to change within us.

Prayer, surrendering the situation, and asking God questions will lead us to the root cause. It will also present an opportunity for us to deal with the root cause rather than continuing the hamster wheel, hoping to go in a different direction, only to find ourselves not progressing in the areas of life in which we are stuck.

We may experience one or more of these at one time, or they may be spread out. Some of these defining moments may occur more than once. Defining moments can be as a result of our bad or uninformed decisions, bad or uninformed decisions on the part of others we depend on, the ups and downs that come with life that we can't control, or they were used as a divine leading to something for a purpose only God knows.

I continue to stress the importance of seeking God for clarity as you navigate this book. The appropriate response to God through surrender and obedience as you pray and fast is essential to your success. If God has led you to defining moments you are or have experienced, there is no need to pray for the situations to change because He has you in it for a reason. He will show you. In His timing, He will lead you through to the other side victorious!

As promised, here is a list of potential defining moments we may encounter in life. Please be advised that this list is not exhaustive nor is this by any means a way to discount a moment in your life that is not on this list but still caused you to change trajectories, your mindset, and your way of being. If it impacted you in a major way, then it is a defining moment.

List of Defining Moments

Marriage

New Baby

Divorce

Change in Careers

Infidelity

Lay off From a Job

Going back to School

New Position in Career/Ministry

Ministry Calling

Physical/Emotional/Sexual Abuse

Death of Loved One

Abortion

Loss of a Friendship/Relationship

Move to a New City

Entrepreneurship

Discovery of Life Purpose

Financial Loss

Change in Relationship Status

Leadership Abuse

Betrayal

How many of the circumstances listed above have you experienced?

How much time have you spent after these experiences to:

- evaluate what happened and what you needed to take away from each experience
- evolve through learning, purging, and preparing,
- elevate to the next level or new season in your life, redefining and moving into the new position with grace mercy, forgiveness, excitement, gratitude and a positive and expectant attitude

Probably not much time. You did what you had to do to keep going, move to the next thing to keep from falling apart, and probably repeated some of the same decisions and found yourself back in a situation once again. Been there, done that!

That's not God's plan and it shouldn't be ours either. But in order to avoid some of the same pitfalls, we have to practice the 4 P's.

Note: Some defining moments may need more than 21 days of Prayer and Fasting to endure maximum chances of success. Please my friend, be obedient to Holy Spirit as He guides you. God wants you to be successful, and I do too!

Position

After reading the section on position, what new information, knowledge, and understanding has God revealed to you regarding position?

Based on the answers to the previous section on prepare, what position are you currently in physically, emotionally, spiritually, and mentally?

Is your current position in alignment with where God wants you in this season of your life?

Which scripture about position spoke to you the loudest?

Create a prayer outlining your favorite scripture to use during your fast.

CHAPTER FIVE

JOURNALING: HOW TO USE THIS BOOK

To begin, you should settle into a quiet and uninterrupted area that is conducive to you being free to do whatever needs to take place during your time with God and for you to hear Him as He guides you.

It is important to set the atmosphere. This can be done by any means you deem necessary, such as introducing music or some form of praise and worship or you can praise and worship without music. If you want to really *go big or go home*, you can light candles, or whatever else you think will be important to your 21-day journey.

If you have one area that you are focused on, then the 21 days will be concentrated on that one area. You will probably find, however, that more areas will be revealed to you as you dig in so be flexible and open to what you hear and observe. You don't want to miss anything.

If you know starting out, that you have a few areas to deal with, then you can focus on one each day. One or more areas may require you to spend extra time on them, so feel free to take an additional day or two pressing into that area. And as I stated before, new areas may be revealed to you, so yield to God as He guides you through the process.

During your journaling, you may need extra space to record all of your thoughts and revelations so be sure to have more paper with you to do so. Record everything! God speaks, and He is eager to show you things along the way so write everything, no matter what it sounds like. Capturing it allows you to go back to read, study and extract your blueprint for success.

I'm extremely excited for the new things God is going to do in and through you so get ready and open your arms wide to receive, receive, and receive!!

4 P's Day One   **Date:** _____

What I'm praying for or about today:

_____

_____

_____

_____

_____

What I need to purge:

_____

_____

_____

_____

_____

_____

_____

_____

I am preparing or have prepared by:

_____

_____

_____

_____

_____

_____

My new position today is:

_____

_____

_____

_____

_____

_____

4 P's Day Two   **Date:** _____

What I'm praying for or about today:

_____

_____

_____

_____

_____

What I need to purge:

_____

_____

_____

_____

_____

_____

_____

_____

_____

I am preparing or have prepared by:

_____

_____

_____

_____

_____

_____

My new position today is:

_____

_____

_____

_____

_____

_____

_____

4 P's Day Three   **Date:** _____

What I'm praying for or about today:

_____

_____

_____

_____

_____

What I need to purge:

_____

_____

_____

_____

_____

_____

_____

_____

I am preparing or have prepared by:

_____

_____

_____

_____

_____

_____

My new position today is:

_____

_____

_____

_____

_____

_____

4 P's Day Four   **Date:** _____

What I'm praying for or about today:

_____

_____

_____

_____

_____

What I need to purge:

_____

_____

_____

_____

_____

_____

_____

_____

I am preparing or have prepared by:

_____

_____

_____

_____

_____

_____

My new position today is:

_____

_____

_____

_____

_____

_____

_____

4 P's Day Five   **Date:** _____

What I'm praying for or about today:

_____

_____

_____

_____

_____

What I need to purge:

_____

_____

_____

_____

_____

_____

_____

_____

I am preparing or have prepared by:

_____

_____

_____

_____

_____

_____

My new position today is:

_____

_____

_____

_____

_____

_____

_____

4 P's Day Six   **Date:** _____

What I'm praying for or about today:

_____

_____

_____

_____

_____

What I need to purge:

_____

_____

_____

_____

_____

_____

_____

_____

I am preparing or have prepared by:

_____

_____

_____

_____

_____

_____

My new position today is:

_____

_____

_____

_____

_____

_____

_____

4 P's Day Seven   **Date:** _____

What I'm praying for or about today:

_____

_____

_____

_____

_____

What I need to purge:

_____

_____

_____

_____

_____

_____

_____

_____

I am preparing or have prepared by:

_____

_____

_____

_____

_____

_____

My new position today is:

_____

_____

_____

_____

_____

_____

_____

4 P's Day Eight   **Date:** _____

What I'm praying for or about today:

_____

_____

_____

_____

_____

What I need to purge:

_____

_____

_____

_____

_____

_____

_____

_____

_____

I am preparing or have prepared by:

_____

_____

_____

_____

_____

_____

My new position today is:

_____

_____

_____

_____

_____

_____

_____

4 P's Day Nine   **Date:** _____

What I'm praying for or about today:

_____

_____

_____

_____

_____

What I need to purge:

_____

_____

_____

_____

_____

_____

_____

_____

I am preparing or have prepared by:

_____

_____

_____

_____

_____

_____

My new position today is:

_____

_____

_____

_____

_____

_____

4 P's Day Ten   **Date:** _____

What I'm praying for or about today:

_____

_____

_____

_____

_____

What I need to purge:

_____

_____

_____

_____

_____

_____

_____

_____

_____

I am preparing or have prepared by:

_____

_____

_____

_____

_____

_____

My new position today is:

_____

_____

_____

_____

_____

_____

4 P's Day Eleven   **Date:** _____

What I'm praying for or about today:

_____

_____

_____

_____

_____

What I need to purge:

_____

_____

_____

_____

_____

_____

_____

_____

I am preparing or have prepared by:

_____

_____

_____

_____

_____

_____

_____

My new position today is:

_____

_____

_____

_____

_____

_____

_____

4 P's Day Twelve   **Date:** _____

What I'm praying for or about today:

_____

_____

_____

_____

_____

What I need to purge:

_____

_____

_____

_____

_____

_____

_____

_____

I am preparing or have prepared by:

_____

_____

_____

_____

_____

_____

My new position today is:

_____

_____

_____

_____

_____

_____

_____

4 P's Day Thirteen   **Date:** _____

What I'm praying for or about today:

_____

_____

_____

_____

_____

What I need to purge:

_____

_____

_____

_____

_____

_____

_____

_____

I am preparing or have prepared by:

_____

_____

_____

_____

_____

_____

My new position today is:

_____

_____

_____

_____

_____

_____

4 P's Day Fourteen   **Date:** _____

What I'm praying for or about today:

_____

_____

_____

_____

_____

What I need to purge:

_____

_____

_____

_____

_____

_____

_____

_____

I am preparing or have prepared by:

_____

_____

_____

_____

_____

_____

_____

My new position today is:

_____

_____

_____

_____

_____

_____

_____

4 P's Day Fifteen   **Date:** _____

What I'm praying for or about today:

_____

_____

_____

_____

_____

What I need to purge:

_____

_____

_____

_____

_____

_____

_____

_____

I am preparing or have prepared by:

_____

_____

_____

_____

_____

_____

_____

My new position today is:

_____

_____

_____

_____

_____

_____

_____

4 P's Day Sixteen   **Date:** _____

What I'm praying for or about today:

_____

_____

_____

_____

_____

What I need to purge:

_____

_____

_____

_____

_____

_____

_____

_____

_____

I am preparing or have prepared by:

_____

_____

_____

_____

_____

_____

My new position today is:

_____

_____

_____

_____

_____

_____

_____

4 P's Day Seventeen   **Date:** _____

What I'm praying for or about today:

_____

_____

_____

_____

_____

What I need to purge:

_____

_____

_____

_____

_____

_____

_____

_____

I am preparing or have prepared by:

_____

_____

_____

_____

_____

_____

My new position today is:

_____

_____

_____

_____

_____

_____

4 P's Day Eighteen   **Date:** _____

What I'm praying for or about today:

_____

_____

_____

_____

_____

What I need to purge:

_____

_____

_____

_____

_____

_____

_____

_____

I am preparing or have prepared by:

_____

_____

_____

_____

_____

_____

My new position today is:

_____

_____

_____

_____

_____

_____

_____

4 P's Day Nineteen   **Date:** _____

What I'm praying for or about today:

_____

_____

_____

_____

_____

What I need to purge:

_____

_____

_____

_____

_____

_____

_____

_____

I am preparing or have prepared by:

_____

_____

_____

_____

_____

_____

_____

My new position today is:

_____

_____

_____

_____

_____

_____

_____

4 P's Day Twenty   **Date:** _____

What I'm praying for or about today:

_____

_____

_____

_____

_____

What I need to purge:

_____

_____

_____

_____

_____

_____

_____

_____

I am preparing or have prepared by:

_____

_____

_____

_____

_____

_____

My new position today is:

_____

_____

_____

_____

_____

_____

4 P's Day Twenty-One   **Date:** _____

What I'm praying for or about today:

_____

_____

_____

_____

_____

What I need to purge:

_____

_____

_____

_____

_____

_____

_____

_____

I am preparing or have prepared by:

_____

_____

_____

_____

_____

_____

_____

My new position today is:

_____

_____

_____

_____

_____

_____

_____

ABOUT THE AUTHOR

C. Jai Graham is dynamite wrapped in a small package. She **is passionate, purposeful, and persistent** in all that she does. She is a Freedom Fighter and Authenticity Advocate. Through the power of her own presence and life, she authenticates and activates others to walk in total freedom and ownership of who they are authentically.

Jai unleashes others into their destiny- a life of purpose on purpose. She is a connector, a launching pad, a cheerleader and supporter. She balances her kindness and empathy with a strong dose of loving truthfulness and drive to provide solutions. Jai is a visionary, possessing both creative and analytical ability.

She is an author, entrepreneur, speaker, facilitator, LifeStyle coach and consultant. Through the concept and practical application of her 3-word formula for success: Evaluate. Evolve. Elevate, Jai's overall life mission is to make everything and everyone, their own kind of beautiful on the inside and the outside.

Stay connected at:
www.mformasterpiece.com
info.masterpieceseries@gmail.com